SEARCHING FOR THE LIGHT

By Joe Kunz

Copyright © 2025 by Joseph Kunz

Cover art by Jem Jarrett

All rights reserved.

No part of this book may be reproduced, stored in a retrieval system, or transmitted in any form or by any means—electronic, mechanical, photocopying, recording, or otherwise—without prior written permission of the author, except for brief quotations in reviews.

First edition 2025

Dedication

This book is dedicated to Abuela Luna and her team of volunteers at El Portal de Luz. Her knowledge, dedication, and wisdom taught me how to connect to myself and the world around me. Thank you for helping me discover the beauty and joy this life has to offer.

This book is also dedicated to my parents, Michael and Margie, for giving me life. My mother embodies the ideal example of a healthcare worker, and is one of my inspirations for wanting to attend medical school.

To my five siblings, Justin, Julie, Jessica, Jen, and Jaq, for supporting me along the way.

To the Benavides family. Roslyn and Victor, you both helped me develop my creative voice through music, and set aside many hours to help edit these poems. I cherish that time, and I'm incredibly grateful to see the love and care you give to your newborn daughter Victoria Rose.

Lastly, this book is dedicated to anyone feeling disillusioned by the world around them, and are seeking for something greater. This book searches for harmony within this dissonance, and finding joy between seemingly rigid lines. In documenting the changes I've experienced in 25 ceremonies, I'm hoping these ideas will resonate with you, and give you hope.

About This Book

This is a collection of poems, ideas, insights, and lyrics written over a span of about 2 years. I wanted to document the transformation and growth I am achieving through ceremonial healing as honestly and directly as possible.

Many poems and ideas were reflections of a dissilusionment of a world that feels too busy to be compassionate. Too cacophonous to find peace, and too profit-driven to provide compassionate care to people who are struggling.

I wanted to lovingly challenge the ideas I once held closely. I wanted to evaluate how much truth this feeling had to it, and transform this struggle into action.

I also wanted to highlight the sacredness of ceremony, and express my gratitude to be invited into a sacred space. It is a process of growing respectfully and humbly, while simultaneously empowering myself to achieve things I never thought possible.

This book is the bridge I've been building to my true self. It connects my individual past, my ancestral past, and keeps me rooted in the present.

This book encapsulates the start of my journey towards healing; the process of deep questioning and connection to this existence.

It is a reflection of my path to the light.

Earth Day

I used to feel like I had the weight of the world on my
shoulders, carrying this burden everywhere

I now recognize that the weight of the world is
beneath me
Supporting me
Strengthening
Nurturing
Loving

It's also high above me
In Giant redwood forests, collectively using might
And their height
To greet the sun

Centuries of patient growth
deeply rooted in the Earth
Existence so seemingly effortless from the outside

My mind opened when I felt the earth breathing for
the first time
Living beings unify in exhale
Gently reminding me to take a moment
To breathe
The Earth tells us how much she loves us

Flora
Fauna
Wildflowers along the journey of a steep incline
With us every step

My parents still remind me of my first step
It's a momentous occasion in our development as
human beings, and often goes overlooked beyond that
recognition

Those of us lucky enough to be born with the ability
to walk
Or to maintain that ability to the present day
Inevitably stop counting our steps

There's no celebration of our thousandth step
Our millionth
Our billionth

The earth reminds us that every step is a celebration
A joyful reminder of our continued existence
The mundane doesn't exist in light
The synthetic doesn't coincide
With the immeasurable power of this Earth

Each step we take is a choice
I choose to walk with gratitude,
With honor
With love

Every breath I take is a celebration
Because it is a gift from my ancestors
A gift from this earth
And a gift I give back to the trees

Reciprocity for this gift of life
All of the Earth's colors
All of the Earth's love

The Calm/The Storm

The calm before the storm
Isn't calmness at all
Moments of tranquility
tainted by anticipation

The seas tell us
Prepare now
Then, settle in

Enjoy these moments of tranquility
Of calmness, of peace, of love
Carry them with you
Into the storm

Flow like the waves beneath you
Open up like the rainy sky above
Embrace the mystery in the clouds
In our ever-changing cosmology

Storms come and go
Danger rises and falls
It will always be out there somewhere
But don't let the storm in the distance
rob you of the here and now

The only time that matters is the present
Let anticipation and worry melt away
Be the peace at sea
Be the calm within the storm

When high seas on the horizon
bring worry and doubt
Recognize the darkness is in the 'there and then'
I am here and now
My light will shine through any storm

Love is not a garnish

It's not something we can top off
And simultaneously bring into existence after the
process has begun
When we're finally comfortable enough to feel
It's not simply a plant we pick to add extra texture

It's the roots of the plant itself
The roots that connect it to the Earth
Connect us
It's how we pick the plants
How we stretch out our hands
Our intention during the process
Our purpose

Far too long, I've underestimated the simmer
Far too long, I've been more concerned about how the
end result may look
Instead of getting lost in the process
Instead of loving for myself

I give my body permission to feel
To open my heart to feel love
I recognize its omnipresent nature
Its perpetual presence
Its generations of song and dance

I give my mind permission to find its beauty
To whisk away clouds of despair
To rid myself of gloomy clutter
Inhaling open skies and fresh air

I give myself permission to feel
Without expectations of what that will be
My fear of love has held me captive
But now I set myself free

The plant that grows the garnish doesn't grow for our
consumption
Its sole purpose isn't to be on our plate
It grows because of its natural process
To branch out
And reach towards the healing sun

Growth is natural and organic
It's necessary to reach peak height
By digging deeper into the soil
While simultaneously taking flight

Remaining open
Is different from waiting
I must continue growing
And letting myself heal
remaining open
And feeling what I need to feel
Continuing to love without expectation

But because its existence
Of not holding out hope
But merely hoping
Hoping that I heal
That we can heal
I hope we find the love deep within ourselves

Because drought hasn't destroyed our beauty
And though flash floods have brought us pain
I see the strength in our foundation
And our growth through all the rain

What if we feel what our bodies want to feel?
What if we give ourselves permission to heal?
Without expectations

What if we nourish that love
And tend to it gently?
What if we water it
And let it grow?

Imposter Syndrome

If every sound is born into silence
And dies into silence
Who am I to break this silence?

What do I want to say?
What's worth expressing in that moment?
And when that sound finally ceases
Does it do justice to the space around me?

Who am I to pick up sticks?
Who am I to strike a chord?
Who am I to seek these forms of expression?
What accolades do I need
to accurately express what's in my heart
In my mind
Who am I to speak over the silence of the mountains?

These mountains knew me before I enter their space
These mountains know my spirit better than I do
They remind me to stand tall
Stand up straight
Shoulders back
Humbly prepared for the world

It's not a matter of speaking over the mountains,

It's responding to their call to join in

The river shows me not to run from something
But to flow towards a greater purpose
Water flows within me
Life coursing through my veins

Who am I?
I am human
I am Earth
I am the rivers that run down the mountain side
I am the stars in the nighttime sky

The Earth simply teaches me who I am
How to become who I'm meant to be
How to have courage, join in, be brave, and have faith
In myself and in the process

Our Earth makes me all of these things
And sends constant reminders to express what I can

*"But remember my son,
Do it with love"*

Catacombs of Choquequilla

*I wrote this poem at Ñaupa Iglesia in the Sacred Valley, Peru.
Three Q'ero elders brought me to the cave's entrance, and
informed me this cave is used to connect to one's ancestral past.*

If an eye for an eye
Makes the whole world blind
We've been stumbling in the dark for centuries

Bloody knuckles and balled fists
So much time spent scraping our hands against rocks
We seem to have forgotten how to
peacefully open our palms

To reach out with love
To feel through the catacombs
To help guide our species out of darkness
And into the light

These catacombs connect us to our ancestral past
The cave gives us a chance to recognize where our
ancestors come from

Where they've been
And maybe why they couldn't continue
It gives us a chance to greet them lovingly
To walk beside them
And if they've had missteps,
We're given the chance to rectify them
To forgive them
To keep our palms open
To pick up where they left off
In our collective search for the light

They can guide us with knowledge
Knowing which routes led to success
Showing us which routes led them astray
So we can walk a slightly different path
Together

They teach us that we're not just walking for
ourselves
We're walking for them, for the ancestors before them
And we're walking for our children
and our children's children

We walk mindfully
to ensure our children walk with peace and love
from the start
So that when they walk the catacombs
There's nothing to forgive

The skin from our bloody knuckles heals over time
Any scars remind us to react calmly, patiently
They remind us to open our palms
Knowing the light is both outside and within
May our children know this light from origin through
the work that we do

Shadow Work

A Thread

When hanging on by a thread
It's hard to show gratitude
The twine of my being seemed so weak
Dangling over the void
This thread is taut
Weighted by everything at stake
It's an anomaly something so thin
Can stretch but not break

Curiously, I look inside the thread
To discover it was woven in the stars
Giving me inspiration to not just dangle and sway
But to climb towards the sky

As I journey closer to the sun
He gives me more energy, more life
The sun passes down another thread
This one made of light

I lovingly wrap this thread around the first
As I reach out for more threads to combine

I wrap reddish love around
So it's tightly intertwined
I wrap around purplish peace
To calm a frantic mind

I sew in green
So I too, may absorb the sun
I grab every bright color
As they slowly set me free

Rolling hills show me
How to wrap the Earth around
How to rise upwards
As I'm supported by the ground

The threads branch upwards
Weaving time and space
So I climb and climb
To find a beautiful place

The fabric of spacetime
conjoin to here and now
The gravity pulls it all together
and the stardust takes a bow

I pull my cosmology around me
Like a weightless blanket
Carrying these threads
Everywhere I go

We can never be truly isolated from others
The world won't leave us stranded
A quadrillion strands of DNA
Uniquely woven

Bound together to create beings
infathomably complicated
And simply human

These strands are woven
In every blade of grass
Reaching towards the light
Ingrained in chloroplasts

If the meadow invites me in,
I leave my shoes at the door
I show gratitude for their messages
Without ever wanting more

How else do these plants persist
despite centuries of violence?
They continue to exist
Waiting in peaceful silence

Their life and power
Practitioners deeply intertwined
Their lessons of resilience
Teaching us how to be kind

Threads meticulously interweaved
Seamlessly intertwined
Sprinkle in the stardust
to help molecules bind

In every rock and atom
Lies peace for us to find
I harness strength from this planet
To release any doubt inside my mind

Ants

She dropped her cupcake, now riddled with ants
Tears in her eyes, she said,
"I can't cross the sidewalk"
The ants are going to eat me."

Part of me held back laughter
Part of me felt her pain
Part of me wondered how often I hold a similar fear
That prevents me from doing the simple things

"Don't worry. You're safe. Do the things you need to
do. The ants won't hurt you, they're our friends."
I guess I was speaking to both of us

I thank the insects for the important work they do
For another opportunity to be aware
Another step towards letting go of fear

Cyclebreaker

Far too long
I've carried this weight passed down through time
The shadows seeped in
They took control of my limbs and my voice

I take these heirlooms
Passed down by some men
Pull them from my overweight backpack
And shatter them with rage against the Earth

My blood boils like a biblical sea
My throat scratches with angry words
My hands ball into fists as I lose control
Finally standing up for myself

But this isn't power
This is weakness
This is calling plays from the same playbook
An arena where I am the same
The pendulum perpetuates ad nauseam
Back and forth through time

I am not that
I am not that anger
I am not vengeance
I am not rage
I am not going to shout at the defenseless
And think it makes me powerful
I take a step back,
and am lightyears beyond this cycle
Brought up by the cosmos

I am a cyclebreaker
I am the roots of the Earth
I am life
And one day may be a creator of life

When that day comes
I'll gently hold that responsibility
I'll hold my child lovingly
And will always be there for them

These shadows don't stand a chance against my love
This violence is no match for my open heart
I clutch the light and shine it into my ancestral past
Blinding the shadows
It burns the demons and transforms them
into something beyond
It sends them to the sun where they become light

I shine this light into my present

I pull it from the sky and blanket my body
Extinguishing rage
Cutting ties so there's nothing for these
spirits to feed on
I shine my light onto the page
as a written contract
Declaring I will never become the monster
it seemed destiny was creating

I am infinite love
I have a responsibility to end this nightmare
So my children only dream peacefully
So they don't have to wait until they turn 33 to
embrace their inner child
So they don't have to redo so many things
to have the life they deserve

I apologize to these ancestors
for shattering their heirlooms
For not holding apsects of my identity near

Picking up these pieces doesn't serve me
I don't need to carry their weight
But I shouldn't have reacted in rage
This feeling in my chest needs a home

I offer the shards to the Earth
I bury them deeply and lovingly
So that future generations can walk peacefully

without getting hurt
I offer them as a token of appreciation for this life
I cover them with soil
Placing them as close to the Earth's core as I can
to these ancestors who brought harm
Because they were brought harm
We all know you could do better

But despite your faults,
I thank you for so many things
Thank you for giving me life
For showing love in the ways you could
however limited

I plant seeds amongs the shards
I nourish them with water
I gently watch over them
Until green greets the sun

I do this
So that we may start over
So that we may sprout a new life
Ending a tired cycle and replacing it
With one that illuminates our consciousness

One that does justice to the beauty of this human
experience
One that celebrates the light of the world

White Coat

Why is healing treated as a luxury?
What's the price of admission for living a full life?

I've had some white coats treat me well
I've had some fail me

One put mints on my pillow
Healed through luxurious retreats
In searching for something more
I fell into a trap that costs tens of thousands of dollars
False promises made
That gave me false hope

In hindsight, I realize I was already on my way
To the healing I was seeking
But on any worthwhile journey
Someone will always have their hand out
Trying to make a quick buck

I've spent so much time questioning why I went
Why I paid so much
Sleeping at a rest stop until it's paid off
Let the traffic noise and car alarms be a reminder
Recognition that I don't need someone's accolades
To know my path towards healing is legitimate
To know my invitation to ceremony is enough

Give me a plot of dirt and let me work
I don't need much more than water and the Earth
To learn how to heal
How to become the healer I'm meant to be

For so long, I had one arm tied behind my back
Let's see what can be done now that it's free
How do I serve my community
Knowing the power in a fair chance?
The pain when someone in a place of power
doesn't uphold their word
I promise to uphold mine

I bring myself love every day
so that I may work with love
I grow stronger every day to support people when
they need it the most
I stay open because I know healing is symbiotic

When I wasn't healing, this retreat told me I'm not
strong because I don't eat meat
Don't underestimate my strength
Don't underestimate the journey that
brought me here
Don't underestimate how my spirit peacefully
navigates this world

May I never underestimate anyone's strength
I won't know everyone's journey
But I'd like to learn as much from them as I can
I know they have their own light within
Their fire that burns
Their power that is either prevalent
Or yet to be discovered
If they haven't discovered it yet
Let us collect kindling
But first, let us ask permission to help
this person realize who they really are

I have a responsibility to help those like me
To help those who are very different from me
I do not take it lightly
I respect and honor them
Humbly

I will treat them with light

Overthinking

My mind keeps wandering off
I'm afraid it will stray too far
And get lost

My body and I are trying to relax on a lush, green field
And instead of relaxing, we end up chasing it around
for hours.

My body is upset.
"Can't we take a break?" he asks.
"No, not until we bring the mind back," I reply.

My body grows weary from climbing over rocks and
along the cliff side. He keeps pleading and trying
to reason with me, but I insist we keep running and
pushing through the pain.

I follow my mind through the weeds, and my body
steps on a thorn. As he tries to remove it, my mind
gets further away.

I say, "Please stop running, we can't do this any
longer."

My mind replies, "Why would I come back? Look at how you're treating my friend."

I allow stillness and soreness to settle in. I feel each ache and pain, every scrape and scar.

How have I neglected this part of me that does so much? I fail to recognize its labor and continue wanting more. I've ignored so many subtle messages that carry wisdom from the Earth.

I speak to them both softly, "I'm sorry for what I've done to you. I hope you can forgive me. If we all reunite, I'll treat you with more love and care."

They're hesitant, but ultimately agree. My mind sends signals to my body, and my intuition decides whether to respond. We lay in the grass until we're greeted by nightfall.

For the first time since I can remember, we rest without worry. We're reunited under the stars.

"Despite everything going on in the world..."

That unfortunate mantra of modern life
gives me an overwhelming feeling
The sense that sitting peacefully
Eating an apple
Overlooking the sea
A moment seemingly tainted by the suffering
humans inflict

I hear a child giggle in glee
as her mother teaches her to greet gentle seafoam
I'm trying to stay present

But I'm simultaneously reminded of the children
screaming in Gaza
Parents digging through rubble and ash trying to get
to their daughter before it's too late

I shed tears for hundreds of thousands of
children, women, and men being killed or injured
As if those tears will soak through the earth
providing any kind of relief

It's naive to think the tears we pour out for Gaza
could somehow seep into the ground
Watering crops on Palestinian soil
Growing food to pick between bomb blasts

It's naive to think that good intentions can build a
missile defense system in Kyiv
Can soak up the blood in Karkhiv

Can prevent a father or mother from being shot in a
routine traffic stop

Tearing apart families who came here
seeking a better life

But it's naive to think that we're
powerless against this system
It's easy to become jaded
to put on a fake smile
to scream at someone in traffic
to become part of the monster

It's much harder to love
But, I'm trying
I've long felt anguish for those on the receiving end of
a bullet
For those exposed firsthand to the horrors of war
And now, I'm trying to find love for those who pull
the trigger
Who order the strikes
Who build the missiles
Who fly the drones

Who couldn't find their power
And instead bond with darkness because they were
never shown light
I'm finding love for those who perpetuate these cycles
And it's easier for me than most

I've never been shot at
I can go to work without wondering whether
unmarked vehicles are going to detain me

I feel for those who destroy because they want power
Who inflict violence searching for something
they will never find
Because destruction and division are the antitheses of
power
They pull us from the light and from each other
Violence pulls us from who we are
From the sanctity of our lives
The beauty in our minds
The love within our hearts

Despite everything going on in the world, I celebrate
our world every day
I celebrate those subtle signs of our cosmology
I'm searching for more compassion
I'm searching for the light in everyone, even when it's
hard to find

Transformation

Joe Kunz

Don't Go Into That Part of the House

No restful sleep
The ceiling may collapse
Attic pitter patter
The rats are running laps
The living room
becoming anything but
Mostly a space for dwelling
as the shutters stay shut

This place isn't a home
I feel too confined
Clutter in the corners
Cluttering my mind

But there's space in the shutters
A gap in the blinds
Hope beyond the horizon
Invitation from sunshine

The light is asking for an invitation
to be allowed in
The rain rapping at my rooftop
The wind chiming in

They're asking if I'm too busy
to notice the dew on the plants
Whether I'm too somber
to get up and dance

As I slowly join their chorus
Movement like concrete
Nature's crescendoing symphony
Lighten my feet

I open all the shutters
Every window and every door
Nature started as a whisper
Building to a roar

I climb into the attic
To tell the rats they cannot stay
They once had a place here
But today's a new day

I dance upon the floorboards
Not minding if they creak and sway
I start laying a new foundation
Building it day by day

I head out to the garden
and pull the weeds from the Earth
Breathe life from the flowers
Fresh air
Rebirth

I decorate my space
Once claustrophobic and confined
I open up my heart
I open up my mind

Though I could get by
Having places I couldn't go
That existence is limited
It's time for me to grow

I sit peacefully
Open space to roam
What was once a dwelling
Is now my loving home

A Symphony

The birds were chirping throughout the
Andes mountains
I wanted to better understand their song

I think he's singing in 5/4 time
then another joined in
Elaborate syncopation I couldn't quite count
I started tapping the rhythm
I grabbed a notebook attempting to transcribe
I started counting the space in between

Water dripped from flowers
The rhythm was somewhat steady but it didn't match
the song of the birds
It was a beautiful texture that fit seamlessly but I
didn't know how to write it down

I started searching for the key but nothing matched
my ear
The tempo was ever changing but soothing
I'd scribble a note, scratch it out, then start again

In frustration, I put the pen down and closed my eyes
I let the soundscape pull me in
I shut off my thinking mind
My desire to analyze what was happening

I connected to my breath for hours
Then reached a moment where the song made perfect
sense

This song is available on major streaming platforms.
It's the first track on the album Blooming by my former band
Cherrystone

Ulysses
Friendly faces in unknown places
Not what they seem
Sirens sound surround and shroud
In this celestial dream

Now her song brings me closer
Impure allure she sings
Drawing near, things unclear
when that pendulum swings

Twisted beauty beckons
I hear them call out my name
Approaching a place of reckon
All to chase a manic state

In the distance, I see the siren
she lies upon the cliffside
finally found where she was hiding
Amongst jutting rocks and riptide

Dysphoria dances in the tightrope
High above the crashing waves
But the beauty of life's water
Washes the darkness away
Pain doesn't persist
In the healing power of the wind
I follow the path of love and light
As a new course begins

I gain higher distance from the ground
Flying high as an illusion I am chained and bound
But I see a new path
just beyond the horizon
one far away from the peril
of a short-sighted siren

This path of growth is the true path to power
We must give ourselves time to blossom and flower
To let our roots grow more deeply
Rooted in resilience and self-sustainability

Socrates

When I stumble upon madness
It's hard to not feel grandiose
Like it's the essential ingredient
that's evading me the most

And though I know it's poison,
I add teaspoons to my well
Increasing drop by drop
and manifesting hell

What happens when your foe
is something fight and flight can't leave behind?
How do I run from a monster
that exists inside of my mind?

For years I fought this monster
Tensed muscles, clenched fists
I felt the pain he caused me
without questioning why he exists

I build a wall of numbness
and a moat of self-neglect
I uproot my garden's beauty
while getting defenses set

And in being war ready
I blocked out all the light
not realizing that the darkness
Powers the monster's might

For years, I suffer
For years, I question whether I have the
strength to keep going
To keep fighting
Dropped to my knees once again

But when kneeling on the earth
I notice that the seeds, once sewn in my garden
continue to sprout
A reminder of how beautiful life is
How beautiful the Earth is

As the flowers blossom
and warmly greet the light
They teach me the path to freedom
That this isn't a fight

I ask them,
Is the difference between Angels and Demons
the place we give them to reside?
What food and fuel we feed them?
Grant their power in our minds?

Is this shadowy figure really here to inflict pain?
Or did I not have the ability to fight on my own
so I manifested a mighty frame?

 If I have the power to create demons
then I have power to create angels, too
Divinity has been here this whole time
I've had the strength this whole time

I look in the monster's eyes
and speak with affection

Thank you, my friend
In my suffering you were born
You're my guardian angel
I just never specified the form

I give you all the courage
All the kindness I can bring
You only exist as a demon
because I never gave you wings

So today I give you wings
I give you all my love
Darkness is no longer within us
It's time for you to rise above

You were my protector
I needed you in my life
You carried me through turmoil
and warded off the strife

I'm grateful for your existence
Your presence I adorn
I release you to the sun
As I plant flowers in your horns

But I mistakenly thought
That you are me, and I am you
But as I grasp my power,
I recognize that isn't true

My power comes from this Earth
From the wind, the rain, the sun
And there was a time I needed you
but we both see those days are done

You're built for war
but I don't need to fight
You're a being of darkness
And I, from Love and Light

One day you may revisit
and if I see you again
I won't treat you as an enemy
I'll greet you as a friend

My friend, thank you for the assistance
But it's time for you to go
Have a beautiful existence
Please get the hell out of my home

Reflections

I often lose sight
Of how far I've come
Forgetting the journey
In daily mundane

Grounded by those
I've known for a while
Warmly greeting eyes
or a genuine smile

Small steps grow
Over many years
And the journey's reward
Slowly becomes clear

Not cursing the weather
While walking through the rain
Revisiting and prepared
With a new mind frame

It lets me appreciate the old
While welcoming the new
A reflection in a puddle
Greeting morning dew

Micro adjustments
Weaving through time
Forgetting each thread
Is cherished as a sign

A sign of old wounds
Slowly healing
And heart opening
Ready for feeling

For being present now
Being present here
Reflecting in stillness
As the image settles clear

Body
I asked my body, "Who are you?"

I am Time
I'm rooted in the present
I am always here and now

Sometimes, I'll send sensations
It's up to you to respond
To determine if it's something worth acting on

If you ignore me too often, I'll stop sending signals
Or I'll turn them up so high, they can ruin your day

Let me run
Set me free
If I want to shake, let me shake
If I want to stay in the sun, you need the rays

I am time
I am the Earth's wisdom
embodied
I am the stars, the moon, the sun

I am the rivers in the valley
I am the sun painting a purple sky
I am the wind who rustles through the forest

I originate from galaxies humans will never see
I am a vessel built to navigate this beautiful world

I am to be cherished
I am to be respected
I am to be loved

I am to be treated as the miracle that I am
With the same sacredness I hold

Stop telling me I'm imperfect
Instead, listen to my instructions
so we can be free

Stay here
Don't drift foward and backwards through time
This beautiful body who floats in the current

This beautiful body that is mine

I am not a cycle

The stock price of toughness is soaring
It's perpetually overvalued and misunderstood
Increasing quantities, increasing inflation

Of the ego
Of the expectations of masculinity
Aggression is stockpiled and tested
the Marshall Islands won't forget

Left Right Hook Block Body Shot

How many weapons have been created since the
dawn of consciousness?
How many opportunities to heal have been hindered
by heavy-handedness?

How much is strength falsely conflated with
destruction inflicted outwards
blocking our light within?

How many mothers have shed tears?
How many children live in fear
and remain unprotected?

From violent cycles
Spirals mistaken for forward momentum
When the spinning makes us dizzy
Too drunk with disorientation
We stumble East or West
because we've lost sight of the sun

We forget these bones, sticks, and stones
Do not belong to us
They belong to the Earth
Draped around the sun

Our father sun is powerful
Not because of his potential to destroy
Instead, he has unbridled power for all life we know
to harness
Lending a hand to all organic life
How he holds our solar system together
With astronomical force so great
Yet perceived so gently on Earth
How he brings us warmth and light
And ensures the moon has equal time and space to
operate in her own way

So I step towards the sun
And let him wash worries away
My cells awaken in the light
They begin dividing and healing
Blood circulates through my veins

Joe Kunz

I've felt something missing
And as I heal each part of myself
I'm rebuilt and rejuvenated
Better than before
Reconnecting with parts of myself
Once shut off while growing weary from the journey
now illuminated

Not wielding like a sword
nor yielding to harsh words
I fully embrace myself
Man enough to recognize the faults many men
perpetuate
Courageous enough to heal

One day, ready to start a family
Ensuring trauma cycles stop
Ready to be an anchor
Ready to be a rock

My body is not a weapon
These hands aren't made to fight
They're made to open up to the Earth
And open my heart to Love and Light

I am not a cycle
My power is to uplift
To be the man I know I am
To appreciate this gift

Community

Dedicated to important people in my life. It's certainly not an exhaustive list, but I wanted to express gratitude for some important people in my life. I also wanted to process some of the lessons that these people have taught me

Amanda

I'm sorry people in your life
Have spent a great deal of energy
Trying to make you feel weak
Trying to tear you down
Trying to make you feel like you are powerless

You have a beautiful ability to walk between worlds
To continue to love despite everything
To bravely dig roots into rocky soil

Despite their best efforts
I know these people can't convince you that you're
powerless
You're powerful beyond recognition

So long as your heart is beating in your chest
You have power
So long as your lungs fill with breath
You have power
So long as you continue to love
You have power

And so long as you continue to grow

You connect with that power

The healing power of the Earth supports you
Your community supports you

As you dig your roots in more deeply
As you continue to grow
It inspires us all

You're on the verge of connecting to your true power
Your true abilities
Keep growing in love
Keep growing in light

Abuela Luna

As you complete another rotation around the sun
You continue having a gravitational pull
that echoes the stars

People often find you at night, singing to the moon
Joining a chorus that's always there
Connected enough to hear nature's songs
Wise enough to know your place on this Earth

You are a harbinger of the light
You understand it and respect it
Sharing it with everyone you can
Spreading beautiful knowledge from the Great Spirit

In the 1,000+ ceremonies you've led, how many lives
have you touched?
How many people have you given the opportunity to
make real change?

At my first ceremony,
you kneeled down to offer guidance and support
It was difficult since your body was stiff in the cold
I realized you will do this work as long as possible

Even if you may not be able to stand back up
But if someone needed help
You'd still help them

You have wisdom as old as time approached with
youthful exuberance
You have an unparalleled ability to connect
To put things into perspective
To ward off the darkness, and connect to the light
To read the situation, and act with love

Anytime I feel restless
I hear your voice shine through
"Patience mijo, patience."

When it rains, you've taught me to thank the rain.
When it's windy, you've taught me to say "Thanks for
showing up for us today, brother."

No matter how many times I thank you, it will nev-
er seem like enough. Since I've known you, you've
helped me grow immensely.
From losing hope to finding joy and love.

Gracias por todo, Abuela Luna
Amor y Luz

Here's to many more journeys around the sun

For Amelia

You visited me in my dream.
You walked into a restauraunt
I walked in to tell you how much I had missed you.

I was going to tell you that life is simple
Love is simple,
and we've made it too complicated.
I was ready to say, for the first time, that I love you.
But in this dream, you were kissing another man.

You noticed me walk outside, and you followed. We
sat under a dimly lit streetlight.
I told you how I felt, and you listened warmly, kindly.
I felt your heart and realized how much I miss you.
I've been thinking about medical school and the
future so far in advance I neglected to tell you what
you mean to me.
That I love you and see a bright future together.
In this dream, the man walked outside.
He was kind and respectful. He had no clue who I
am.

The man in the dream was kind of a dork, but

was good to you. He treated you gently in the
way you deserve. He asked me about med school.
"How long are you in school?"
"What kind of medicine do you want
to practice?"
I got so dizzy with a barrage of questions.
I told you, "I'm so sorry I missed my chance."
In the dream, I noticed you were a few weeks
pregnant, and instantly woke up in a flurry

I texted you at 6am scheduling a time to chat. My
dream told me that I have an urgent message and I
needed to tell you before it's too late.

You were out hiking with friends, but this time, the
video was shot from a higher angle
 When we finally connected,
you confirmed you're seeing someone else.
"Estoy saliendo con alguien..."

I realize that I'm too late, but still want to deliver a
message to you
Thank you, Amelia.
Thank you for the best date/camping weekend I've
had. Thanks for being adventurous and beautiful.
Thanks for being brave and independent.
Thanks for bringing me joy and driving 7 hours to be
my +1 to the wedding.

I'm sorry things didn't work out, but
thanks for showing me how to love.
Thanks for teaching me that when the right woman
comes along, there may not be second chances.
That I need to live in the moment and
stop worrying about the future.
Things will work out when I work hard and stay
open.

Love will find a way when it's nourished.
When it's treated as sacred.
I hope you can build the future with this man,
or whoever you end up with.
I hope your children can visit
the ranch where you grew up.
I hope they can play in the dirt and
pet your horses.
I hope he can meet your dog, Lucky.
I hope you both have the future I thought about so
often, but was too fearful to speak about because it
felt too soon.

I hope he's the man who shows up in your dreams.

I know I'll be fine, better than
fine. I'll meet a woman sometime soon,
and we will explore outdoors.
She and I will fall in love and build a foundation.

We can do this because I learned the consequences of not being open. I learned to live in the moment and to be spontaneous.

I learned that the right woman deserves me to be the courageous and loving man that I am

You're teaching me how to let go without resentment.
How to take the first chance I get instead of asking for another
You're teaching me how to be open
from day one so that I never have
to write the last poem.

Te amo mucho, Amelia.
Disfruta tu vida
Disfruta tus relaciones
Disfruta su amor
You deserve the world.
Te amo

This poem is dedicated to Joe DeRose. I was ready to quit drum-
ming due to overuse injuries. He worked with me patiently to
completely change how I drum. He taught me to play with more
patience, feeling, and joy

The Drum
I held onto the drum too tightly
Out of desperation for direction
The stick couldn't breathe
The heads couldn't sing

Letting insecurities of the mind seep into purpose
Blocking out the joy and why I play
It became about not being good enough
Instead of getting better

The body showed signs of stopping
Playing through hours of pain
Thinking I was on the path to greatness

I now know the body was sending messages
That this wasn't the way
Gravity is powerful
But the ego thought I needed more force

In a way, I'm learning to harness the power of the sun
To let gravity do the work
Because if they're put into this form for my use

I'd better be respectful of their sacrifice
Feel at the forefront
Coaxing into a groove
Where expression melts limits
Time constructs rhythm

Where my heart does the talking
Blocking out chatter in the mind
Where the relationships are symbiotic
Cymbals resonate back
They teach me about momentum

Once chained to the drum
I connect to its liberation
To the availability of expression
Of joy, love, change, and beauty

Every time I strike a drum
I do so to hear
What message resides inside
Every time I strike a drum
I hear my mentor
I hear those who have come before
Who have made the instrument what it is

I see those who I teach
I see the smile when they connect to the sound
The frequency resonating through time

Gabriel and Raquel's Wedding

In the evening of one of my first ceremonies, I was
learning to trust those around me

Raquel sat peacefully, with a cup of green tea on her
ringless left hand
Natalia, who was about 5 years old, wanted her
mother's attention
She put her hand inside her mother's hot tea

I expected scolding
A response of anger and frustration
I saw a glimpse of this reaction, then Raquel's
expression quickly changed

Her eyes softened
She picked the now crying child up
Put her on her lap
Hugged her tightly
And kissed Natalia's slightly singed hand

What beauty
Nourishment
And strength

What an opportunity to teach how
the healing power of love
Is spread through action and compassion

Like when Gabriel takes them to the waterfall
He lovingly picks her up
Lovingly picks us all up
With movement
With dance
With energy so contagious, you're forced to smile
Planting pines and moving the energy
stuck inside of others

How beautiful that these two are united
How beautiful that Abuela Luna is the one to preside
and give her blessings
How beautiful to create a bond of eternity
In a life with no beginning and no end

How beautiful that her loving left hand
Is adorned by a ring
To represent that eternal bond

Searching for the Light

Seeing the Light

Self-care isn't comfort and luxury
It isn't just a fancy vacation
Delaying the mundane

Finding the light takes time
A deep search within to unlock my true self

This self was shrouded by shadows
Finally learning how it feels to be safe
Recognizing every misstep
Not hiding from it
But holding it up to the sunlight to examine why
Forgiving myself
Forgiving others

To find the love deep within their hearts
Recognizing their humanity is
deeper than these actions
Recognizing whether I contributed to this treatment
somehow

It's been the hardest thing I've ever done
but undeniably the best
To finally step into a realm where I was once
swarmed with shadows

Where I used to be overwhelmed with fear
Instead, speaking kindly, and boldly,
"I'm here to work. You know where to find me. I ask
you leave me to work in peace, because no matter
what attacks you bring, we both know I will defeat
you."

I returned to my past self with love,
comfort, and warmth
Instead of being frustrated he didn't do more
I realize he did all he needed to do at the time
to get to the here and now

To uncover inner strength and courage
That was buried deep inside
Coming back each month to find what's next
To open myself up to the full spectrum of emotions
Refusing to withdraw from the energy around me
even though it's easier to hide

I learned how to stay open despite the
suffering in the world
Understanding that when people lash out
It isn't them
It's the shadows hiding their true selves

It's the humility to recognize I couldn't help others as
much as I'd like
That I was too overstretched in their energy
That knowing this comes from a good place
That I need to put my oxygen mask on first
And breathe in the fresh air

One of the greatest gifts has been the invitation to sit
in loving ceremony
To receive unconditional aid from those who have
come before
To find collective healing
Freedom from the shadows
Rebirth into the light

What a powerful feeling to be asked to help others
After 16 ceremonies
Immense growth, overcoming setbacks, ill-disciplined
regressions
To find change beyond my wildest dreams
To finally be offered the chance
To lend a helping hand
To play a part in this journey for others
As I simultaneously stay focused on my own

To think that maybe things have been so hard
for a reason
Battle-tested inner peace

To mold my heart into that of a healer
To recognize I am so much more than
I previously imagined
To recognize the line where the self ends
and the other begins is simply an illusion

To learn how love and life find a way
To keep transforming, evolving, and healing
To grow in power from this Earth
Blood flows from raindrops
Wind carries the shadows away
The earth holds us tightly
The sun provides infinite light

I am eternally grateful to see the light
I'm eternally grateful for the help along the way
And though I am not fully healed yet,
I'm well on my way

In infinite love and infinite light
We are eternal

Anti-aging serum

There's no such thing as an anti-aging serum
Nothing we can buy
Will transcend time
Or touch the divine

This divinity already exists
within our bodies
within our minds

If you remove the synthetic from cosmetic
Are we closer to the cosmos?
Iron flowing through our bloodstream
Joining us from lightyears away

The cosmos, the stars in our eyes
Always exist in time
We've always been divine

We live in a world that can profit from magnifying
our insecurities
From pointing out the ways we don't fit standards of
strength, beauty, handsomeness, or whatever else we
think we should be
It tells us we're too skinny or fat, or too short or tall
It tells us everything we're not
It distracts us from who we are

We are all beautiful, strong, and everything we think
we're not and ought to be

The number of days I walk on this Earth are limited
And there are so, so many people I wish were still
walking alongside me
          Without worry
          Without pain

It's hard to watch people suffer
It's hard to know our own worth
When worries wash over us
It makes it difficult to breathe
To recognize the beauty of our own breath
To reconnect with our own divinity
When bombarded with distractions
Messages that we're not enough
Searching for a wrinkle in time that returns us to our
nostalgic youth

But let those wrinkles form around my eyes
They're a reminder of my continued privilege to walk
this Earth
I hope they grow larger
Unbridled and unmitigated

Our signs of aging are merely the growing textures of
our own existence
They shouldn't be shunned with the artificial
But worn as a beautiful badge of honor
      A commitment to our continued divinity
      Our infinitely meaningful existence

If your insecurities are ever tampered with
If your beauty goes unrecognized
Feel the strength of the world beneath your feet
Recognize that you're enough
You're more than enough
You're powerful far beyond your own recognition
We're all powerful beyond our recognition

We are art
We are harmony
Abundance
Prosperity
We are love
We are all light

Daylight Savings Time

I often cursed daylight savings time
Winter cuts days shorter

I now realize the moon is just greeting me earlier
She has a message she wants to share
She too, wants to illuminate the sky

Lake Shastina

I swim in Lake Shastina
Thanking the water for its beauty
the beauty of this life
I owe it to myself
and beings outside of myself
To not be pulled away from this moment
                    Of peace
                    Of calm
                    Tranquility
                    Good company

The water reflects how far I've come
Overcoming fear of floating where my feet can't reach
Overcoming an inability to trust these senses
That pull me one way or another
Away from the light
The water has memory of the past
My body is rooted in the present
Together, they navigate these sacred waters
Keeping my mind from wandering into the future
Thank you for the journey
Thank you for the present
Thank you for the beauty of the moment
Thank you for the beauty that is yet to come

Driving

I'm driving down the back roads
Through a winding path towards the unknown
Fear wants to drive
cautiously and predictably
Taking the off ramp to familiar places
Instead of forging ahead

This fear was never derived from the light
A plant attempting to grow in the shade
It's time for me to take control

Fear, take your hands off the wheel
and step out of the vehicle
I'm sorry but this is your last stop
We're leaving you here

It's time to let courage drive
To lovingly head into the unknown without fear
We're heading somewhere new
Where there's no space for self-doubt

Wisdom is in the passenger seat calling out directions
We're forging ahead
Staying present
In love and light
To secure the future I deserve

These lyrics will be included on the EP, Searching For The Light

Take Me to the Cosmos

Why do we stay confined
When we're limitless?
How do I connect
To an existence
Divine
Beyond this?

How do we claim back
what's naturally ours?
Synapses and shooting stars
Our life unconfined
How do we free our minds?

Sea of breaklights
Undertow pulls me in
Father Time
Breaks out the belt again

Getting swept out to sea
The coast feels so far
But I breathe into the ocean
And navigate with stars

It's just within reach
Only out of sight
I grasp it tightly
Grab hold
and take flight
Take flight

Take me to the ocean
I dig my toes in the sand
Waves, timeless cycles
Lessons from the land

Take me to the forest
Where I can just be
Where the wind exhales
As the trees breathe

Show me your mind
How neurons traverse
The iris in night skies
Embodied universe

Take me to the cosmos
Where time begins
Vastness and expansion
The same depth from within

Joe Kunz

Show me the stardust
Strength of infinite suns
Their infinite light
How they and I are one

Fight or Flight

I wasn't born with wings
Should I muster enough strength
Kick and thrash enough to get airborne
My problems would follow me
As soon as my feet return to the ground

No, I was born with feet
They connect my soul to the earth
I was born from love
Into an existence sometimes so painful
It leads me to want to escape
To fight
To look for ways to numb

But I was also born with purpose
I was born into something much greater than myself
A purpose far beyond
I come from many things
To create one seemingly small part
Of something larger

I'm meant to be here
I'm meant to contribute to something greater
And when I lose sight of this
When it becomes hard to breathe
To embrace the overwhelming senstation

That existence is breathtaking
Sometimes, I wish to ride a comet into oblivion
I could wish to be born with gills to hide from
greed in the ocean
But humans are extracting oil down there, too

But I wish to stop wishing
It's time start doing
To continue the path of humble acceptance
To continue walking in the light
To continue becoming myself
To keep changing those things that do not serve me
And embracing those parts that do

Peacefully
Lovingly

As a bird glides peacefully above the ocean waves
I no longer think "I wish that was me. I wish for
nothing more than to be free."

Instead I tell them, "Thank you for being you.
I wish for nothing more than to be me."

The Mountaintop

I was hiking up the mountain
Trying to reach the top for over a year
I plotted my course
Took wrong turns
Got lost
Found parts of myself I had abandoned
Found a connection to nature I never knew

And one day, I felt the ground give out
I turned an ankle
And rolled all the way back down
I know this isn't rock bottom
But damn it feels close

Maybe this happens for a reason
The pendulum's polarity seems like the worst curse
you could give someone
I was told it's a gift
So I kept thinking
"Maybe I'll understand why when I finally reach the
mountaintop."

Maybe I know the course better this time
Maybe there was a flower I didn't see
Or a rushing river I didn't stop to appreciate

Maybe being caked in mud and rainwater isn't an
inconvenience
But a wearable reminder of where I come from

The Earth said "I made these for you, but you didn't
notice. You weren't getting my messages so I brought
you to the ground so I can whisper them in your ear."

Ambition blinded my periphery
I was so narrowly focused on one goal, one task
That I didn't appreciate the interconnection between
everything along the way

Maybe one day I'll reach the mountaintop
Soon, I'll reach new heights, and defeat the things that
ail me
The Earth is teaching me to not conflate the two

I pick myself up
I tend to my wounds, and start again
But this time,
I don't do it out of desperation to heal
Out of spite for the things that keep me down
Or because it seems like the only option

This time, I'll try to notice beauty in everything I see
Savoring nature's staircase
Recognizing each step

As I hike further up the mountain, this time feels
different
This time I do it with love
Love for myself
Love for others
Love for the Earth
Love for the Spirits that guide me
And love for the fact that it isn't actually about
reaching the mountaintop
But savoring each part of the journey along the way

Peaks and Valleys

As beautiful as nature is
Not every view is breathtaking
There isn't a secret waterfall
tucked around every bend

Few moments are spent on the highest peak
Looking over the forest
Mesmerized by the landscape

But this isn't something to look down on
So much of existence
Is neither peak nor valley
But the space in between

Everytime I expect to be awestruck,
Is a moment I let slip away
It's a moment I don't reach out
Place my palms in the dirt
Feeling what needs to be felt in the moment
If I spend my whole life chasing peaks
The spontaneity of existence dwindles
Subduing those somewhat elusive moments
Of pure joy

If I wander mindlessly
I'm sure to get lost in a valley of shadows

Instead, it's teaching me to simply be aware
To ask, without judgement
Why am I here? Was it something within my realm of
control? Am I holding onto something too tightly? Or
not tightly enough?
What message do you have for me? Where can I
search for knowledge so I may leave this place to
continue my path?

I'm learning to be present in every moment
Becoming aware whenever my mind drifts off
Welcoming it back gently
Speaking to it like a wandering child trying to make
sense of the world

I'm doing my best to not let moments slip away
This life is something I cherish greatly
The mundane has no place amongst the stars

The Earth teaches me how to be here
How to connect to my heart
To my power
To others

Now, when I reach a mountaintop
Or watch a waterfall cascade down
I can immerse myself in beauty
In the water pouring from the sky
Bathing in pure light
Because my journey there shows me how to be
mindful of every step

There's no place for shadows inside my beating heart
I send you to the sun, so you can transform into
something new
I scan every corner of my chest, to see if there's
something you need to tell me
As you depart into the daytime sky

There's only space in my heart
To be fully here
To be present
To be grateful that this beautiful heart keeps working

Life is easier in the light
When I recognize that beauty is everywhere
When I recognize the power
Of this open heart

I'm hoping these poems create a dialogue between my earlier self and my more healed self. I wrote grey a few years before Snow Angels, expressing my struggle through Portland's gloomy winters.

I wrote Snow Angels in response to that past self, and how I navigate gloomy seasons now

grey

When blue skies turn drab and dreary
And the grey skies overstay their welcome
Everything dampens

When the eyes of loved ones
don't shimmer like they did before
When the songs of birds don't sing quite so
beautifully
It's okay to not feel the same way
If you can't connect to the light, don't force it
But don't let the shadows tell you that
the light is no longer there

Recognize it's there
Recognize how it's helped you
And how it will continue to help you

Camp out under the stars
Let the clouds roll over
Batten down the hatches
Anchor the rain fly and, if it's all you can do
Ride the storm

Because tomorrow is a new day
The greens, blues, hazels and brown in everyone's
eyes will resurface
The mountain will stand in the same place
And you'll be able to connect again soon

Just have faith
Don't force it
Appreciate the beauty when it comes

Snow Angels

Mercury drops
I pull my comforter over me as freezing temperatures
kill my motiviation to go outside
I guess it's just another winter to hunker down

Snowfall buries ambition
I shutter the doors and windows
And as I close the blinds,
I see a family gleefully sledding down the hill

This winter is different!
I run outside and throw myself into the fresh snow
My spine aligns in sensation
My body is so cold, it burns

I feel every sensation
My arms flail up and down, up and down,
No regard for perfection
No place for judgement
I realize I'm making a snow angel
Laughing at how a grown man making snow angels in
his pajamas may be perceived

Joe Kunz

The gloomy clouds part ever so slightly
The sun pokes his head through
He tells me, "It's going to be a beautiful winter."

A winter to create something imperfect and fleeting
To express this beautifully complex existence
To appreciate the moment
It won't last forever

Becoming the Light

Floodgates

Open the floodgates!
Open every hatch
Slide open the windows
And let in
the light

I've weathered the storm
Released fear
Despair
Hopelessness

And stepped into love and light

Open everything
The good, the bad, the unknown
Not to let dark energies in
But to open up fully to this beautiful existence

Other storms will arise
Difficult moments will come
But I open myself fully
Knowing that I can now navigate anything
life throws my way

With love

Thank you to this beautiful process
To this beautiful planet
The beautiful work these beautiful people
have done for me

Thank you to my journey
It's been far from easy, sometimes seemingly
impossible
I've walked so very, very far to be here and now
To the doorstep of triumph
I'll knock with everything I have until it opens
For a chance to step into the light

Sound is Light

Sound is the light we cannot see
Wavelengths that we carry
Reflections and projections

The first radio broadcasts have since made their way
to outer space
A visitor overhearing them may initially be impressed
by our archaic technology
Looking through the window of
human creativity and intuition

How would they feel diving deeper,
back into projected time?
Towards this planet's beautiful surface
To hear cacophony and chaos?
Pivotal moments in history
Caught in the juxtaposition of our state
An appetite for destruction or an ability to create

So many resources are spent on this cacophony
I'm searching for the open space away from this noise
For silence, where peace seeps in
Where the true messages are communicated
In between all of the advertisements

It's easy to forget how it is to be still
If sound is simply another form of energy,
how do we celebrate it?
How do we create, produce, recreate, and share sound
that does justice to our cosmology?
How do I speak in a way that appreciates the
human experience?

Each of us comes from infinite light
We have the capacity to carry infinite love
We must be intentional with the sound we create
With the songs we play
The words we sing

We must paint the landscape surrounding us
Spattering soundscapes that each one of us contains

I need to be intentional with my word
These wavelengths do more than what meets the eye
They bring us closer together, or push us farther apart
I'm done projecting aimless noise into the nebula
I'm speaking from within
I'm starting to choose the moments to share that light
Carefully, upon reflection

Sound is light
Sound is sacred
It needs to be treated as such

I Am Light

As I step into the light,
I realize that life is simpler than we make it
Existence is easy
When approached with love

Thank you for showing me the way
For teaching me that shadows can't live in the present
There's no space for them inside my heart
Even though things have been difficult
The universe is guiding me to become who I am today

Thank you to everyone who has
helped me on this path
Thank you to the Earth for abundance
For each beautiful moment
Every beautiful day

I walk this path peacefully, willingly, and prepared for
any challenge that comes my way

Thank you for these moments of peace
To the infinite stars who sew the fabric of light
across nighttime skies

Thank you to the light, for guiding me,
and teaching me how to work

How to become a servant of the light, and help others
Hard work becomes easier when
fueled by a burning star
Powered by an abundance of love

I walk this Earth peacefully
Humbly
Because I am this world
I am love
Infinite

I am that same light that shines through the universe
Guiding the path towards illumination

To everyone who has helped me along the way
From the bottom of my heart

Thank you

Amor y Luz

About the Author

Joe Kunz is a poet, author, songwriter, and drummer. He hopes to help create an interdisciplinary bridge between healing modalities using evidence-based research, artistic expression, and wisdom shared from ceremonial
healers.

As he continues his own path towards expression and peace, Joe hopes to share insights from a place of humility and acceptance, operating under a framework of life-long learning.

He thanks you for taking the time to reflect on his poetry, and hopes that these poems help you as you search for your own light.